# WALKS v
## in the
# AROUN

# Dennis & Jan Kelsall

## A Questa Guide

© Dennis and Jan Kelsall, 1999
ISBN 1 898808 06 6

Questa Publishing
27 Camwood, Bamber Bridge, Preston, Lancashire PR5 8LA

## ADVICE TO READERS

Readers are advised that while the authors have taken every effort to ensure the accuracy of this guidebook, and have been required to revisit all the routes during the course of preparing the book, changes can occur which may affect the contents. The publishers would welcome notes of any changes that they find.

This guidebook has been compiled in accordance with the Guidelines for the Writers of Path Guides published by the Outdoor Writers' Guild.

**Also by Dennis & Jan Kelsall**

Walks with Children in the Lake District: Ambleside & Grasmere

**and by Dennis Kelsall**

The Pembrokeshire Coastal Path
Discovery Walks in Warwickshire

Printed by Carnmor Print and Design, London Road, Preston

# Contents

# *Introduction*

Occupying the head of the River Kent's lower valley, Kendal lies in a fold of gently rolling terrain, where constantly changing horizons bring novelty to the scene with each step. Nowhere does the surrounding land attain any great height, yet contour and position are everything and are often exploited to perfection, with panoramas that are as beautiful as they are expansive being revealed quite unexpectedly.

To the north of Kendal, the hillocky landscape is characterised by becks and streams, weaving through a disorder of low hills, to merge with three rivers that have broken free of the mountains to converge above the town: the Sprint, the Mint and the Kent itself. Sinuous valleys, dark waterfalls, boggy hollows and lush water-meadows each have their separate charm and invite the discovery of a more intimate landscape. As the Kent runs away towards its estuary to the south, it loses none of its spirit or its capacity to delight. Wooded banks still hide foaming cataracts and winter floods can produce a spectacular sight. Here, the indefinable softening in the surrounding countryside has its own appeal, with much to see in the hedgerows and ditches.

To the west, the ground rises along an uptilted limestone slab that culminates in an abrupt longitudinal cliff overlooking the Lyth Valley. From there, your attention is drawn to the distant western hills or across the vast expanse of Morecambe Bay and, as your eyes drop across the plumb-straight criss-cross of ditches, excavated when the marsh was drained, they fall onto the woodland border below a cliff.

The area has a rich history, extending back more than two millennia to a time far before the Romans arrived. Each age has left its mark in earthworks, castles and settlements and in the pattern of fields and paths that bind them together. So too, the farmhouses and village cottages, many of which are very old, although often utilitarian in their construction, incorporate features of special interest such as mullioned windows or the massive round chimneys which are so distinctive of the area. The relics of past industry are also evident. From the 14th century,

Kendal prospered through the manufacture and trade of woollen cloth, but many other industries have also been important, such as the production of felt, dyes, timber and wood products, flour, paper, leather goods and gunpowder. They all relied on power derived from the fast-flowing and plentiful rivers and streams and, over the years, as many as thirty separate mills lined their banks. A few remain as buildings, but elsewhere, traces can still be seen in broken weirs, overgrown leats and ruined walls.

Perhaps the single most important fillip to the area since John Kempe established the weaving industry in 1331, occurred in 1818 when the Lancaster Canal was extended into the town. Although primarily built to transport coal in and stone out, the canal created ready access to an area of abundant raw materials and freely available water power. Together these supported the development of a range of new industries, including the manufacture of carpets, shoes and ropes and the production of snuff. Its heyday was short-lived and, unable to compete with the railways, the canal fell into disuse and, sadly, parts of it have been filled in. But, you can still see its two most impressive features, an aqueduct at Sedgwick and a tunnel that carries it arrow straight through the hillside at Hincaster.

Kendal itself remains a vibrant and individual town, not single-mindedly pandering to the whims of tourism or totally engulfed by unimaginative and wearisome retail and commercial development. Old buildings with new purposes, local shops and businesses offering personal service and wonderful food, are all there to be appreciated. Wander through the old alleyways and courtyards enclosed by the clusters of houses and workshops that were built to accommodate the growing woollen industry. Visit the parish church, probably unique in having five aisles, climb the hill to the castle or, on a rainy day, take refuge in the town's museums and galleries.

A final point, although parking is available at or close to the start of all the described routes, not all of it is within recognised car parks. You should, therefore, ensure that your vehicle is parked sensibly and safely and not causing an obstruction on the road or to farm and field accesses.

All that now remains is for you to go out and enjoy yourselves.

# 1

## Bowston and Staveley

*Encrooked within a bend of the Kent, south of Staveley, the countryside here assumes an air of ruggedness occasioned by bare rocky outcrops that protrude out of the pastures. You will see few other walkers and there is much to enjoy in this little corner.*

**Total distance: 5 miles**
**Start: A slip road beside the A591, about 1 mile north of the A5284. GR485964**

1   Towards the northern end of the slip road, take a footpath, signed to Bowston across the field on the right. Exercise care crossing the main road on the other side and walk away down a narrow track opposite, past cottages to a railway line. Over a bridge, the track follows the line to the right towards Bowston Farm.

2   However, before getting there, turn left through a gate and walk across the field to a stile in the far wall. Beyond that, keep going in the same direction to another stile in the far corner, coming out at a junction on Winter Lane. Cross over and follow the minor lane opposite down to the River Kent and on to Cowen Head. Walk beyond the old paper mill, now an apartment complex, and through a handgate on the left, just before reaching some cottages.

3   Climbing gently behind the cottages, the track leads through a kissing gate into the corner of a fellside pasture. Walk on a diagonal to a stile in the top far corner and, maintaining the same line, cross a sparsely wooded hilltop, guided by a vague trod and an occasional marker post. You shortly reach a wall stile leading to a small garden at Cragg Farm. Walk across to a gate and follow a drive down into the farmyard, there bearing left to leave again through a gate adjacent to an outbuilding. A field track climbs

around the edge of a wood to a pair of gates. Go through the right-hand one into a larger field, and walk on, picking up a line of power cables to a stile in its far right corner. From there, an enclosed track leads eventually to the road, south of Staveley.

### *Staveley*

*The market charter it received in the 13th century evidences that it was an important place in its day. Its prominence continued, as in 1538, a school was founded in the village and in the 19th century it was regarded as the major bobbin producer in Westmorland. Of interest in the village is the church, originally put up in the 14th century and dedicated to St Margaret. Following its rebuilding in the 19th century, it was rededicated to St James and only the tower of the earlier structure remains. It contains a splendid stained glass window designed by Burne-Jones and manufactured by the William Morris Company, which depicts the Crucifixion and Ascension.*

4   Turn left and walk to the level crossing, leaving the road immediately beyond it through a gate on the right, from which a track runs alongside the railway into a field. There turn left, walking across to a stile on the opposite side, emerging at the main road. Take care crossing over, then climb another stile directly opposite and follow a track, leading to a cottage. Immediately before reaching the fence, which encloses the cottage, turn off to the right, rising to and then following a wall to a stile in the distant corner of the field.

5   Keep going over that, heading towards Ashes Farm, which can now be seen in the middle distance, to cross another stile. Now walk diagonally left to a track, beside the far wall coming up from the farm. Turn left, following the wall – not the track – to a stile in the corner, which leads into Ashes Coppice. A clear path winds through the trees. At a fork further on, bear right and walk down to a ladder stile and out to a field.

6   Follow the continuation of the wood on your left, keeping going beyond to pick up a trod across the heath. After passing through a gated opening, the way reaches a broken section of wall, where you should turn left to follow it to the field corner. Cross a stile into

the adjacent field and walk away with the wall on your left. Maintain the same direction across successive fields, later picking up a grass track, which leads you out to a lane, Crook Road.

7   Turn left and at the next junction, go left again into a lane (Ratherheath Lane). After about one-third of a mile, look for a stile over the wall on the left. Walk diagonally across to another stile in the field's opposite corner. Beyond that, follow the edge of trees to the first of two handgates, from which a path winds on through the wood. When you reach a lane (Ashes Lane), cross directly over and keep going through the trees, finally climbing back to the lay-by from which the walk began.

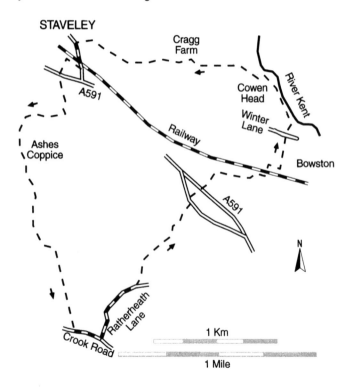

# 2

# *Cunswick Scar to Bell Hill*

*Cunswick Scar is justifiably popular for the views it affords, but the field paths and ancient lanes below its foot are frequented by few. The high point of the walk (in terms of altitude) is at the start, and inevitably, this means a climb to be encountered at the end of the day, but don't be put off, as it is well graded and not too strenuous.*

**Total distance: 6 miles**
**Start: Car park at the top of Underbarrow Road, between Cunswick and Scout Scars. GR488923**

1   A track from the road past the transmitter mast leads to a path through a small wood and out to the rough fell pasture beyond. Follow the perimeter wall around, keeping ahead at a crossing path. At the end of the wall, bear left, still following signs to Cunswick Fell. After crossing a stile and, later, a kissing gate, descend into Scar Wood, following a path across the escarpment to a track at its base. After a stile, the continuing path leads to another kissing gate and out of the wood. Walk directly across the field and scale a stile into the corner of a small plantation. Go ahead along its edge to regain the fields on its far side.

2   Now turn left towards Cunswick Hall, shortly meeting a tarmac track. There, turn right through an opening in the fence and walk across the field to a now redundant stile. Beyond that bear right to lose height and pursue a field track down a bushy bank to the bottom of the field. Walk ahead and over a stile, following the hedge on the left to a squeeze stile. Cross through and turn right to continue on its opposite side. In the next field, walk to the far opposite corner and go through the marked wooden gate. Keep your line through the ensuing field, crossing to its far corner, where a field track goes left through a gate to Fell Gate Farm.

3    Go right to walk around the farmhouse and out through a gate, there forking left onto a field track rising into rough pasture. Keep on, soon picking up a fenceline on the right, which will guide you out to a track (Capplerigg Lane). Turn left and then bear right at a fork to pass behind Capplerigg Farm, shortly coming to another fork in the track, in front of Bell Hill. Now branch left and follow the track down hill. After crossing a stream by a slab bridge at the bottom, the track bends to go through a gate and into a field. The way remains clear, the track climbing to a junction, where you should bear right and walk down to a gate, the way now being signed to Underbarrow.

4    Through that gate, the track is again enclosed and, after abruptly turning left in front of a second gate, narrows to rise over an un-named hill. At the far side, the path drops to a junction, there go straight over, now on a metalled way. Further on, after passing a track to Cold Harbour Farm, the way rises to another junction, where a bridleway (Gamblesmire Lane) leaves through a gate on the left. Follow this as it leads over a low hill and drops to enter a small wood before climbing through it and across open fields. Eventually it is joined by a track on the left coming from Cunswick Hall, but our way continues ahead. Later, the track bends, passing a lime kiln over to the left, before rising to a final gateway.

### *Lime Kilns*

*The end of the 18th century saw many developments and improvements in farming practices, one of which was the widespread use of lime to sweeten acid soil. It was produced in kilns, such as the one here, by baking limestone to yield quicklime and then adding water to give the slaked lime used on the fields. Lime kilns tended to be built, either where the limestone was available, or else where the lime was to be used, on the farms. They were cleverly designed to minimise labour, generally being built into a hillside so that they could be easily loaded at the top and emptied from the bottom. Alternating layers of broken limestone and culm, a poor quality coal, were dropped above a layer of brushwood, which was then lit and the whole allowed to burn until the reaction was complete. Once cool, the lime could be broken out from the bottom and carted away.*

*Similar practical elements of design were incorporated in local barns, also often built into a hillside. The hay and fodder could then be brought in from the fields to be stored on the upper level and then, during the winter, easily dropped to the cattle pens on the lower floor.*

5   Through that turn right, retracing your steps beside the wall to the wood and then back to the road.

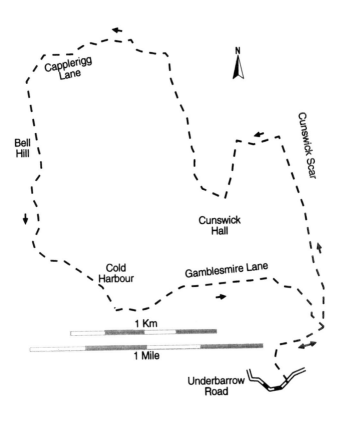

# 3

# *Helsington Church from Kendal*

*This walk ascends the high ground that separates the southern reaches of the Lyth and Kent Valleys, from where there is a wonderful view along the estuary to Morecambe Bay. Returning across the fields the route follows the Kent back to Kendal.*

**Total distance: 5½ miles**
**Start: A6 south of Kendal, just north of its junction with the A591. Roadside parking is possible in nearby residential side streets. GR508907**

1   Leave the A6 along a drive to Lane Head House Country Hotel almost opposite a petrol garage, and signed to Helsington Laithes. Where it divides at the top, go left and shortly pass under a road bridge. Immediately after, turn left again through a gate, follow a track up the right-hand field edge and pass through a second gate. Now strike diagonally across the field to a gate about halfway along the far perimeter.

2   Continue in the same direction across successive fields, heading towards High House Farm, which becomes visible after you crest the hill. In the corner of the third field, go through the left of two gates.

3   Later, when you reach a track, ignore it, maintaining your bearing across the fields to reach a squeeze stile to the left of the farm buildings. Beyond that, keep going, now parallel with the wall to the right, to a final stile and out to a lane.

4   Turn right to pass the farm entrance and climb to a junction at the top. There, go through a squeeze stile into the field on the left and strike across its diagonal. Ascend the next field, passing a

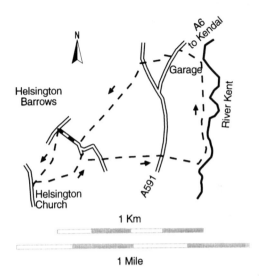

clump of trees. Beyond the crest, Helsington Church comes into view and serves to guide you down.

### *Helsington*

*Although Helsington is a parish and has a chapel and once had a school, there is no village, as such, with the name. The small church, dedicated to St John, and its adjoining school were built in about 1726 to serve the little community of Brigsteer, huddling at the foot of the scarp, and the surrounding farms.*

5   To go back, return to the point at which you joined the lane beside the former school and walk away from the lane, following the wall on your right. A rough track develops a little higher up. Stay with the track until eventually you reach some cottages at Brigg House Farm.

6   Go through a gate in the wall on the right between the first and

second cottages and pass the front of the house on the left to a gap in the bottom hedge. Turn right, pass through a gate into a field and then go left, walking to another gate part way along its far edge.

7   Emerge onto a lane and cross to another gate opposite, where a sign directs you to Prizet. Walk down crossing successive fields and keeping the same direction, until eventually you reach the main road.

8   Cross to the house opposite and go along a track behind it, rising to a wooded bank and ending at a lane. Again, cross and continue along a signed footpath, descending steps beside a garden and into a small paddock beyond.

9   Keep going down, crossing a track to a stile beside a barn and on until you reach the River Kent. Turn left to follow it upriver along successive field edges.

10 Eventually, the path strikes out left across a long field, shortening the river's meanderings to rejoin it at a lane. Go left, the lane crossing a small stream and climbing through a strip of woodland to return you to the A6, almost opposite the start.

# 4
# ℒevens ℋall and 𝒦endal

*Throughout history, Kendal's prosperity owed much to the river running through it, which provided the power to develop the town's multiplicity of industries. But it was the coming of its second waterway, the Lancaster Canal in 1818, that was singular in its effect of modernising the town and, for a 120 years, the waterway was its arterial link with the industrial world. Although both are now redundant to economic purpose, they provide a lovely circular route between Levens Hall and Kendal. Although a somewhat longer walk, there are several links between the two watercourses, allowing you to shorten the route at will.*

**Total distance: 8½ miles**
**Start: Lay-by beside the A6, immediately north of Levens Bridge. GR496852**

1   Walk back towards the Hall, but turn off the main road immediately after crossing Levens Bridge through a gate on the left, signed to Hincaster Lane.

### Levens Bridge
*As in most parts of the country, the names given to local places and features can often create quite a bit of confusion. Here, for example, Levens Bridge crosses the River Kent, but the River Leven actually flows out of Windermere to pass under Newby Bridge. Between the two lies the Lyth valley, and yet there is no River Lyth!*

2   An obvious path climbs above the River Kent to join an avenue through the deer park. Leave it through another gate at the far end and turn left onto Hincaster Lane, crossing a bridge over the

Kendal trunk road. Just over, steps, ascending a bank on the right, lead through a gate into a field. At first, follow the right-hand fenceline out of the corner, and then head for an isolated bridge that soon comes into view. Passing underneath it, its purpose becomes clear, as a drained ditch which was part of the Lancaster Canal is revealed. The onward route now traces its former towpath and the accompanying canal remains more or less evident for much of the next two and a half miles.

3     At Sedgwick, the canal is carried over the road on an impressive stone aqueduct, constructed in the finest traditions of Victorian substantiality. It is worth dropping down from the canal at this point as you can better appreciate the bridge's construction from the road.

### Sedgwick

*Prominent behind the village stands the Victorian Gothic Sedgwick House — its steeply gabled roof and embattled tower reminiscent of a fairy story and harking back to an earlier age. It was built in 1868 by William Wakefield, whose father, John, a Kendal businessman and banker, had established a gunpowder works in an old corn mill beside the river. From these humble beginnings in 1764, the business grew into a successful enterprise with two dedicated mills later being built. Although the family eventually sold the business on, production continued until 1920, employing up to 50 people. The factories have now been demolished, but you can still see remains of the buildings and the water channels hidden along the wooded banks of the river.*

4     Beyond the village, the canal has been filled in, but the walk continues across the fields and beneath a second bridge into Larkrigg Spring Wood. Here, the canal is again well evident, as it has been carried across the sloping hillside as a long embanked trough, which continues on the far side of the wood to another bridge. Although largely filled in again from this point on, the gentle curves of the waterway remain distinct, contouring across the open landscape. Before reaching the next bridge, over which a lane connects Natland with Brigsteer, there is one more short section

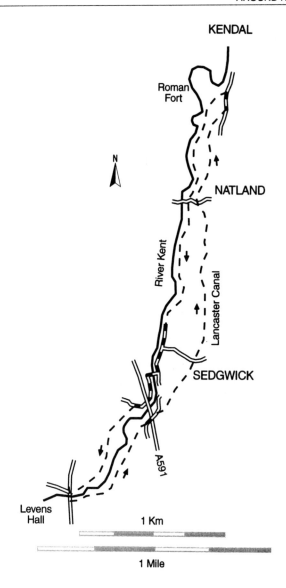

KENDAL

Roman
Fort

N

NATLAND

River Kent

Lancaster Canal

SEDGWICK

A591

Levens
Hall

1 Km

1 Mile

of unburied canal, but after that, its traces are less apparent. Nevertheless, the course of the onward track is unmistakable across successive fields and passes beneath one more accommodation bridge before finally emerging onto Natland Road.

5    Walk ahead towards Kendal but, just beyond a speed restriction sign, turn left onto a tarmac drive to Watercrook Farm. After passing a cottage, the lane widens into a turning circle, where there is a stile on the left. Strike away from it on a right diagonal across the field, making for its far corner by the River Kent. Turn to follow it downstream but, as the water then curves off to the right, keep ahead to find a stile at the right-hand end of a wall by some trees.

6    Now back with the Kent, the way lies along a riverside path that runs alternately atop high banks and the water's edge. Eventually, the path ends at a gate and you come out onto a lane, turn right and walk down to a bridge. Although our way does not lie over it, the crossing provides an impressive viewpoint over the river, which here has cut a narrow gorge into the layered bedrock. The sight is particularly arresting after heavy rain.

7    The onward route lies over a stile on the left, as the road bends round to meet the bridge. Keep following the path downstream as before, either by the river or along a field edge, the way never in doubt. Eventually, after passing a suspension footbridge, the way becomes a surfaced lane. Keep ahead at the first junction, but at the second, turn right to cross the river. Again pause to admire the view, as here there is another series of shallow falls.

8    Over the bridge, a narrow lane on the left follows the river's opposite bank, but has been severed by the construction of a bridge to carry the trunk road high above the water. A cantilevered walkway beneath the span unites the lane's truncated ends, whose continuation leads past cottages at Park Head. Just past them, go over a stile on the left and walk diagonally across the field to another stile in the far wall. Over that continue ahead along the field edge to a final stile into Levens Park. Occasional waymarks indicate the path back to Levens Bridge and the end of the walk.

# 5

# Around the Helm

*South-east of Kendal, rising steeply above Oxenholme is a distinctive hill, The Helm. Although of modest height, its isolation blesses it with expansive views. This walk, along its summit, then encircles the pleasant valley behind, through which runs St Sunday's Beck.*

**Total distance: 5½ miles**
**Start: Lay-by beside the A65 at Barrows Green, near the narrow road onto the Helm. GR526882**

1  Walk south from the lay-by to find a narrow lane, on the left, only a short distance along. It climbs away from the main road, passing over a cattlegrid to run at the base of the open common below The Helm. If you prefer a less strenuous beginning to this walk, simply follow the lane for about three-quarters of a mile to its end. However, more impressive views are to be enjoyed by walking along the top of the ridge and the extra effort of the climb is well rewarded.

2  To gain the ridge, turn right immediately after the cattlegrid along a rising track marked to Stang End. Then, bear left onto a less distinct path that scales the grassy flanks of the hill. Make for the highest point, where you will find a survey trig point.

### The Helm
*Rising in splendid isolation from the surrounding countryside, the Helm is a distinctive landmark for miles around. This vantage was exploited by early settlers to the area who recognised advantages in settling above the boggy forested valleys, where they could see what was happening around them and achieve some security from attack. Around the summit, there are traces of the early earthwork defences that augmented*

19

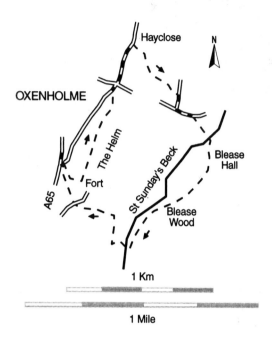

OXENHOLME

Hayclose

N

The Helm

St Sunday's Beck

A65

Fort

Blease
Hall

Blease
Wood

1 Km

1 Mile

- the natural bastions of the site, which was occupied both by
- the native British and then the Romans, when they later set-
- tled in Kendal in about AD 80.

3   Beyond the summit, a clear path follows the wall north along
the crest of the ridge, gently undulating downwards. Further on
where the track and wall part company, stay with the falling track to
rejoin the lane by a second cattlegrid near its far end.

4   Walk on to a road junction, opposite the Station Inn, and carry
on along the continuation of the lane opposite, signed to Sedburgh.
After about one-third of a mile, you will reach the entrance to
Hayclose Farm on your right, turn in at the first gate and go to the
bottom of the farm, through a gate and down to the far end of the

yard. Turn right between a couple of barns and walk down through the gate ahead, ignoring the nearer one on the right.

5   A track leads across the fields, taking you to a pair of gates at the far side of the second field. Ignore these, instead, turn left and follow the fenceline on your right to a field-gate, almost at the bottom of the field. Walk across the paddock beyond, leaving through a gate at its far corner. A track leads past the back of Low Garths Farm and out onto Beehive Lane.

6   Turn right and, at the junction at its end, go left. About 250 yards along, on the right, there is a track up to Strickley Farm. Turn onto it, but abandon it after a few yards, ascending steps and a stile on the left to enter the corner of a rising field. Climb beside the hedge, continuing over the top and down through a couple of gates, making for a footbridge over the stream at the bottom.

7   Bear right to cross the field towards cottages, going through a fieldgate ahead. Leave by a wooden handgate, a few yards further on, on the left, passing between the cottages to come out on a track opposite Blease Hall. Turn right, signed to Bleasehall Wood.

### Blease Hall
*There was a building mentioned on this site in the early 16th century, which was said to be a three storey 'tall house' and occupied by a priest. It is also reputed to have been a pack-horse station, one of the stages along the trade route between Carlisle and Yorkshire where the horses could be changed. The house was later bought by Roger Bateman, who amassed wealth as a wool merchant in Kendal. In about 1570, he extended the house in the Elizabethan style, building the impressive stone mullion and transom windows and frontage that can be seen from the drive.*

8   Walk ahead through a farmyard, bearing right to pass a barn and then leave along a track through the fields beyond. Continue ahead when the track finishes, following the right-hand boundary the length of the field. Through a gate, keep going down the next field, leaving through another gate in the corner. Now bear right,

making for the right-hand edge of the opposite wall, where a wooden slab bridge leads to a ladder stile. Walk on across to a handgate and into Bleasehall Wood.

7   A winding green path leads over a low rise to the far edge of the wood, where a stile by Saint Sunday's Beck marks the exit to the fields beyond. Stride on across the fields, following the stream down for a little under half a mile until you pass a white house, partly concealed by trees, on the opposite bank. Just beyond that, in the corner of the field, ignore the ladder stile ahead and instead turn right to go over a footbridge.

8   Walk up the meadow away from the stream to join a track coming from the white house and keep going ahead, passing through an opening beside a cottage at Stang Green.

9   Leave the track a short distance beyond, going through the first of two gates on the right. Bear right and walk the length of the field to its narrow far end. There, go through the right-hand one of two gates ahead and walk on to find an opening on the left. Through this, climb along the field edge over a hill, passing through a gap into a lower field on the far side. Cross that, bearing left to a gate in its far wall and keep the same direction up the next field to a metal gate in the top boundary.

10 Walk on to a farm track coming up from Helm End and turn right, climbing through trees to reach a lane at the top. Cross to a track opposite, which leads, through a gate, over the southern shoulder of The Helm, returning you to the start of the walk.

# *6*

# *Lambrigg and Docker Fells*

*To the north-east of Kendal, the ground rises above the rolling valley pastureland, giving way to open moorland. The hills are higher and have a feeling of remoteness not found on most other walks in this book and, although they present no difficulty in fine weather, inexperienced walkers might wish to avoid a misty day.*

**Total distance: 5 miles**
**Height gain: 920 feet (280m)**
**Start: Roan Edge Quarry, off the main A684 road, just west of its junction with the M6, there is room to park on the quarry service road. GR586929**

1    Walk back to the main road and cross to two gates just opposite. Go through the one on the right onto the open moor and walk away from the road on a rough track, initially following a fenceline on your left. Where the fence later turns away, keep on going ahead eventually to join a wall on the left. Follow it as it bends left and in about a quarter of a mile, reaches a corner, where there is a gate.

2    Through the gate, walk ahead, bearing away from a wall that runs on your left. The land falls quite steeply to the base of a valley, where a faint track develops to lead you on up the far side. Keep climbing, the track becoming more distinct and eventually levelling off at the top of Docker Fell. The summit actually lies over to the left of the track, close to the wall.

3    The way is then joined by another track from the right and runs ahead, paralleling a wall over to the left. Now clear, the track begins to lose height, turning to run alongside a wall on the left. Lower down, it passes through a gate and is then enclosed between stone walls.

4   At the bottom, turn right onto a lane near Haygarth and walk along it for about a mile, passing an occasional farm. At the end, again turn right. Keep going, shortly passing a junction on the left. A little further on, look for a gate on the right leading onto the open fell. Through that, a track climbs away up the rough hillside pasture onto Lambrigg Fell. It later forks, the more predominant track branching off to the left. However, keep ahead, still steadily gaining height. Further on, a track joins from the left, continue forward, presently to follow the line of a short stretch of wall, over on the right. Beyond the end of the wall, the track soon comes to some ruinous buildings. The summit lies off the footpath, about 300 yards to the left, amongst the tussocky hillocks. Although unremarkable and identified only by a low, rude cairn, the lonely rise gives a fine view over the surrounding moorland.

5   By the buildings, the track bends around to the left, but instead, walk on ahead, passing the top of a shallow, but deepening valley which develops in front of you. Keep straight on, generally maintaining your height on the left side above the valley, until you eventually meet walls from the left and right at a corner.

6   Now return by your outward track to the main road at Roan Edge Quarry. To remind you, go through the gate and follow the wall on your right. After it later curves around to the right, strike away from it at a small angle, following a developing track across the moor. The track shortly joins with a fence on the right, leading you on to the gate at the road.

### Walls and Hedges

*The majority of the drystone walls date from the 18th century, when enclosure for crop rotation replaced the old strip and open field system used since Saxon times.*

*Where the stone or labour needed to build a wall was lacking, hedges were used instead. But without proper maintenance these soon grew out, leaving gaps at the base through which livestock could escape. Simple annual cutting is not enough and, for a hedge to remain effective, it needs to be layered periodically. Although the practice was common throughout the country, different styles developed to suit the needs of each*

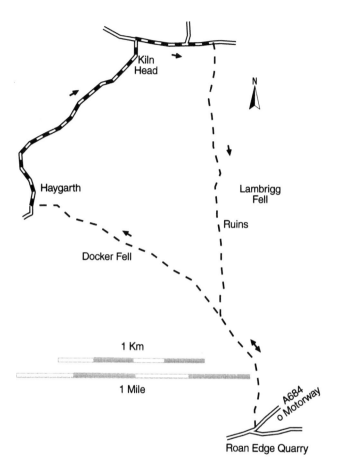

region. Here in Westmorland sheep country, a close, dense hedge is needed and once the superficial growth has been cleared the remaining stems are partially severed near the base and laid horizontally, woven between upright stakes to hold them in place. A hedge like this remains effective for up to fifty years before it needs re-layering.

# 7

# *Benson Knott*

*Just south of Meal Bank, Benson Knott rises as an impressive hill overlooking the River Mint. The walk up to it is neither long nor too demanding.*

**Total distance: 2½ miles**
**Height Gain: 590 feet (180m)**
**Start: Lay-by on the A65 Appleby Road, by the turning off to Meal Bank. GR542953**

1    Walk back along the road over the railway bridge, continuing for about a hundred yards past cottages to find a gate on the right, beyond which a track climbs to a barn. Where the track bends in front of the barn, go through a gate into an open field on the left. Strike ahead without losing height across the slope of the field. At the far side, climb a stile and then walk along a right diagonal to a gully and stream that borders a strip of woodland beyond. Turn right up the hill following the course of the stream, the climb eventually easing before you come to the end of the right of way through a gate in a crossing wall.

2    The summit of Benson Knott lies about 500 yards further on, a trod leading to it from the gate across the open fell. There are in fact two distinct tops joined by a saddle, the one on the right being marked by a trig point and giving a fine view over Kendal to the Lakeland fells. The one on the left, however, is slightly higher and crowned by a well-made cairn.

3    Instead of returning by the ascent route, go back through the gate, and walk diagonally left out of the corner, passing crossing a shallow grassy 'V'. On a clear day, take as your heading the Longsleddale valley, which can be seen breaking the hills of the distant horizon. Take care as you descend, there are rocky outcrops

which are not obvious from above and drop quite steeply. They are, however, easily evaded.

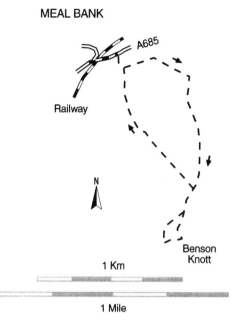

MEAL BANK

Railway

Benson Knott

1 Km

1 Mile

N

4   Make for the indented corner of a stone wall, which shortly becomes visible ahead. Just to the left of it, there is a handgate into the corner of the next field.

Through that, keep going in the same direct-ion, taking a diagonal line out of the corner to reach the wall on the far side. As you follow the wall down, a track develops, leading you back to the barn that you passed near the start of the walk. Retrace your steps to your car.

### Toll Houses

*The house passed on the road is an old toll house. There appeared at the end of the 17th century, to house the pikemen responsible for collecting the turnpike tolls. They are recognised by their projecting windows, which allowed a clear view of traffic along the road, not only to ensure that all dues were collected, but also so that the gate-keeper would have time to have the barrier open for an approaching mail coach, otherwise he was liable for a fine.*

# 8
# Around the River Mint

*The open countryside surrounding the valley of the River Mint is typical of much of that which surrounds Kendal and this walk, starting on its northern side at Meal Bank, samples some of its delights. On the return section, a compass might help you more accurately plot your course across the large open fields west of the Slough.*

**Total distance: 6¼ miles**
**Start: Meal Bank, there is roadside parking nearby.**
**GR539956**

1   Leave Meal Bank along a minor road, climbing north-east towards Patton. About 300 yards past the entrance to Hipshow Farm, the hedge on the right is replaced by a wall in which there is a narrow stile. In the field, angle down the bank to Patton Hall Farm, picking up a track into the farmyard. Bear right to the bottom of it and turn left through a gate between barns. Go out through a second gate to the field beyond.

2   Walk away beside the left-hand wall, continuing on its other side beyond a gate, part way along, shortly reaching a sparsely wooded enclosure. Cross into it, but leave again almost immediately by a stile on the right. Bear left, crossing the fields and later picking up a track that leads you to a farm at Old Field End.

3   Go into the farm and then pass around the outside of the buildings, following a wall to a gate. Through that drop to a second gate and walk in a diagonal out of the corner, following a trod across the fields towards the cottages ahead at Field End.

4   Walk past the row of cottages, turn right onto another track and go beyond the front of the farmhouse to a telephone box at

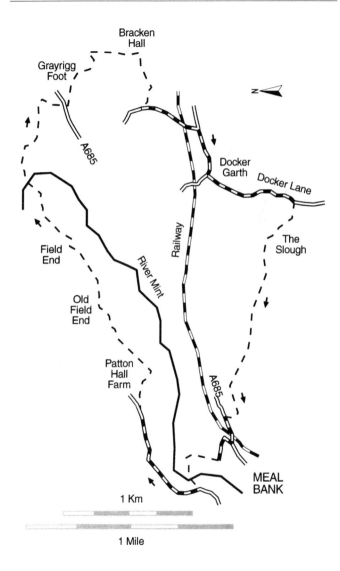

Bracken Hall

Grayrigg Foot

A685

Docker Garth

Docker Lane

Railway

The Slough

Field End

River Mint

Old Field End

Patton Hall Farm

A685

MEAL BANK

1 Km

1 Mile

the bottom. There, go left through a gate and walk ahead, initially beside the right-hand wall, but keep ahead where it later finishes, finally leaving the field through a metal gate onto a track.

### Ash

*Ash trees, which are common in the area and can be easily recognised in early spring by their characteristic black buds, were regarded in country lore as having special powers. Norse legend tells how Odin created the first man from the trunk of an ash, found washed up by the sea. A smooth and particularly strong wood, it was used for many purposes including tool handles and cart frames.*

5   Follow it a short distance to the right, and leave again through a gate on the left, marked 'Dales Way'. A trod crosses to a footbridge at the bottom and then bears right to climb past the end of a wooded bank to the top of the next field, making for a gate to the right of an old barn.

6   Go through to a field track and walk away from the barn, joining and following a hedge on your right to a stile in the corner. Drop down the next field, over another stile and on, eventually emerging through a gate onto a metalled track. Follow it right, out to the road. There, turn right, crossing to leave by a gated track a few yards further on, leading to Grayrigg Foot Farm. Go through to the field at the far side of the yard, walk on to cross a bridge and then pass through the gate, over to the right. Climb alongside a stream to a metalled track running towards Greenhead Farm at the top. Turn left along it, but before you reach the farm buildings, descend a bank and pass through a gate on the right. Walk ahead over a rise, dropping to another gate on the far side. Through that, go right, making for the back of Bracken Hall Farm, now seen ahead. Cross a stile behind the house to reach the farmyard and turn right, passing between two cottages and away on a track. At the end, turn right and walk down to its junction with a lane at the bottom, where you then go sharp left.

7   Although now travelling on country lanes for the next one and a quarter miles or so, they are pleasant and generally quiet.

However, you should take care against approaching traffic.

8   Shortly after passing beneath a high viaduct carrying a railway over the road, you will come to a junction, there turn right. Walk on to the next junction at Docker Hall Farm and go left down Docker Lane, signed to New Hutton. Shortly, after passing underneath power cables, at a bend, leave through a gate on the right, the way being signed to Meal Bank.

9   Bear left down the field to where a plank bridge crosses a stream by the far wall. Go through the gate on the right, just above it and then bear left away from the stream towards the farm ahead. However, ignore the gateway that comes into view, and climb instead to the top corner of the wall on the left. There bear right and walk over a low hill, dropping to a stile in the fence at the bottom. Cross the stream beyond and, with your back to the stile, walk directly away, climbing the rise ahead and then on across the expansive field beyond.

10   Towards the far side, you will meet a crossing track. Go left to join it and, where it then forks, just a few yards on, take the right branch, following it through a gateway in the fence. Keep going, eventually closing with a boundary on the right as you come to another gate. Continue ahead, passing below a small water authority building, to enter the fringe of trees beyond it. On the far side of a brook that runs through them, cross a wall stile and then another stream.

11   Climb the bank away from the stream and, maintaining your earlier direction, walk across the large, open field to a stile in the far wall. Over that, keep going, now heading for a barn, where a gate leads you out onto a stony track. Follow it down to the road. Here turn left, walking as far as a railway bridge, where a lane on the right leads back down to Meal Bank. Part way down, turn off onto a minor track on the right and follow it past houses and then around to the left through a small industrial estate. After crossing the River Mint, it climbs up to the main lane, along which the walk began.

# 9

## Otter Bank to the River Sprint

*There is a veritable maze of field paths and old tracks
within the parish of Skelsmergh and this walk is purely
an excuse to wander leisurely amongst them, the banks
of the River Sprint serving as the objective.*

**Total distance: 3 miles
Start: Lay-by on the A6 at Otter Bank, about 3 miles
north of Kendal. GR531972**

1   Walk up the main road only as far as a narrow lane on the left,
signed to Garth Row. Down there, at the first bend, go through a
field-gate on the left. A green track heads across the fields, shortly
leading past a marshy area. Walk around the far side of it to a stile
in the wall, to the left. Over the stile, carry on along the left-hand
side of a stream, where a grass track develops and bears left,
climbing to a handgate and the main road. Go ahead the short
distance to Stocks Mill, and leave again, turning off along a track
signed as a bridleway to Coppack Howe.

### Watermills
*There is scarcely a river or stream of any note in the area that
did not boast at least one mill beside its banks, harnessing the
power in the water for all manner of industrial purposes. But,
for it to operate effectively, a mill needed more than a fast-
flowing river or stream, the water had to be managed to ensure
that a consistent and controllable supply was delivered to the
wheel. To achieve this, weirs were built across the watercourse
upstream of the mill. From these, leats, or channels, conveyed
the water to the mill, maintaining a sufficient head to provide
the power needed to drive its machinery. When the mill needed
less power or was idle, the flow could be reduced or stopped,
thus conserving the water supply.*

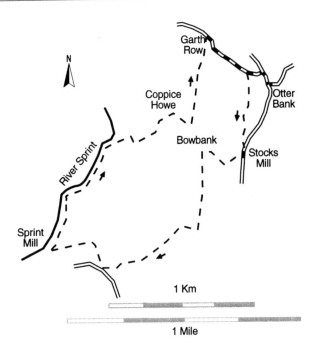

1 Km

1 Mile

*Different types of water mills existed, dependent upon the prevailing conditions and the use to which it was to be put. In the more usual designs, the water was delivered to a vertical wheel and the power transferred through gearing to drive machinery. A simpler arrangement, consisted of a horizontal paddle wheel pivoted at the side of the flow. Only used for grain mills, it obviated the need for gearing as the grindstone sat on the same axle-shaft as the paddle. Mills of this type were less common, but there was at least one on the River Kent.*

2  Cross the stream below the former mill and continue, soon coming to a fence stile on the left above Bowbank. Descend the sloping paddock and out through a gate at the bottom. Turn left again and go through another gate ahead.

3   Follow the foot of the bank on the right above a boggy depression and walk on to pick up a hedge line. Where the field narrows at the far end, negotiate a ladder stile in the left corner. Keep going across the next field and over another stile just right of the far left corner. Now turn right and walk up beside the field edge and through a wooden gate.

4   Bear left across the next field, over a ladder stile in its far corner and continue in the same direction to find a stile in the far hedge. Now follow the left boundary of this and the next field to a wall stile. Beyond that, strike diagonally to the right, crossing to another stile and over a stream and then follow the stream down, and out at a junction of lanes.

5 Turn right along the minor lane to Oak Bank, but just before reaching the cottages there, go left through a field-gate, signed to Sprint Bridge. Walk away beside the wall, crossing to its other side through a squeeze stile part way along, to reach a wooded bank above the River Sprint.

6   When you reach the river, turn right and make your way upstream, the path leading shortly past Oak Bank Mill to a long meadow. Keep going to its far end and cross a disused leat, just below where it leaves the river. Walk ahead, crossing a couple of stiles to emerge on a track. Turn right up to Garth Row Lane and then go left. Within yards, its surface degrades to a track, climbing between layered hedges.

7   At the top of a rise, go through a gateway on the right towards Coppice Howe Farm. After a gate as you approach the farm, bear left through a field-gate and follow a green track to the right, passing the farm buildings before dropping towards a gate opening. However, don't go through, but turn left and follow the field edge to a squeeze stile just before the corner. Over that, go left to a ladder stile and walk on along a vague track above a depression in the field to your right. The farm at Garth Row appears ahead, the route taking you across a small paddock and out through a gate beside the barn. Walk round to the left through the farmyard and leave along a track that ends at a lane. Turn right, back to the main road.

# 10

# Around the River Sprint

*The River Sprint has its source in the wild and remote reaches of the Longsleddale valley, but it is the more gently rolling and open countryside of its lower reaches that is explored in this walk.*

**Total distance: 5 miles**
**Start: Sprint Bridge, north-east of Burneside. Parking there is limited and it may be better to park in Burneside. GR524957**

1   A stile on the eastern side of Sprint Bridge gives access to a field path that leads upriver beside the Sprint. At the top of the field, cross the river by a bridge to Sprint Mill and pass between the old mill and its adjacent cottage. Keep ahead, leaving the track for a path that rises behind the buildings and then turns right to parallel the course of the river upstream.

2   Further on, over a stile, the path parts company with the river and makes its own way along successive field edges. After crossing a stile at the end of the third field, immediately go left to another in the corner. Over that, now turn right and follow the wall to a gate ahead, continuing over the hill beyond. Leave by a final stile at the top right corner.

3   Now on a lane, go left for about a quarter of a mile until you come to a left-hand bend at the bottom of a dip. There, turn off right along a bridleway signed to Mirefoot. Approaching Beetham Bank, the obvious track turns to the right, climbing to the farm. Just before you reach the yard at the top, go left through a gate from which an old grass track rises behind the farm. After a while, it then loses height, bringing you to another farm at Shepherd Green.

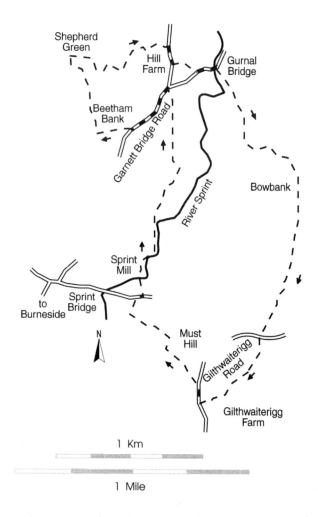

Shepherd
Green

Hill
Farm

Gurnal
Bridge

Beetham
Bank

Garnett Bridge Road

River Sprint

Bowbank

Sprint
Mill

to
Burneside

Sprint
Bridge

N

Must
Hill

Gilthwaiterigg
Road

Gilthwaiterigg
Farm

1 Km

1 Mile

4   There turn right, walking between cottages into a small paddock. Keep ahead, crossing two stiles and then a stream. Go right to follow it, but then bear left to another stile. Over that, walk

around the garden behind Meadow House, slip through a handgate in the wall and out along the drive to a track.

5   Turn right, and walk down to a junction, there going left. At a fork a little further on, choose the way on the right, which terminates at two gates. Take the left-hand one and walk by the wall on the right to a stile in the corner. Over that, bear right, crossing the field to a gate in front of Hill Fold Farm, now visible ahead. Again bear right passing through the farmyard and out to a lane beyond.

6   A group of cottages lies along the lane to the right, where a marked footpath leaves between the last two buildings. Walk through and across the rear garden, to find a stile over the bottom fence. Keep going to another stile and then through an opening at the bottom onto a track. Cross towards the barn ahead, where a stile on the right leads into a field. Now, make for a final stile in its opposite far corner and climb out onto a lane. Turn left and walk down to Gurnal Bridge and the River Sprint.

7   As soon as you reach the far bank, leave by a stile on the right, marked to Coppack Howe. Cross the width of the field to a second stile and ascend the bank behind, where a crossing track leads to a stile into the field at the top. Walk ahead, keeping left of the highest ground, making for an obvious tree beyond the wall at the far side. Continue along the next field, walking almost to the bottom, where there is a stile in the hedge on the left. Over that, walk directly away to a gate in the middle of the opposite hedge and out at a junction of tracks.

8   Choose the track opposite, signed to Stocks Mill, but a little further on, beyond a gateway at the entrance to Coppice Howe Farm, abandon it through a gate on the left into a field. To the right, a green track perimeters the buildings before passing through an opening beyond. Keep straight on, walking beside a small plantation of spruce and then out through a gate to join a track. Bear right, sticking with it only a few yards, to go ahead and through a gate, to the left of the cottage at Bowbank.

9   Keep straight on, following the base of a bank to the right of a

marshy depression, shortly picking up a hedge line. The field narrows at its far end, where you will find a ladder stile in the left corner. Over that, walk to a stile just to the right of the field's far left corner. Now, go ahead, following the left boundary across this and the next field and then directly through a final field, leaving by a ladder stile back onto a lane (Gilthwaiterigg Road).

10  Cross to another stile opposite and strike across a field, making for a wooden powerline post. There, bear right, over a stile in the hedge, and cross a footbridge. Keep going, with the stream on your right, heading towards Gilthwaiterigg Farm, which now comes visible in front of you. A handgate leading onto a track lies just to the left of the low building ahead. Turn right, walk past the farmhouse to its garden at the back. Bear left across the grass, passing through a gap in the wall ahead and walk on past a bungalow onto a road (Gilthwaiterigg Road). Turn right, but then a short distance on, leave again on the left along another track, signposted to Sprint Bridge.

11  At Must Hill Farm, the track winds through a yard before leaving by a gate at the far end. However, instead, go through a field-gate on the left, immediately after the house. A grass track curves around the field edge to pass into the next field. Keep ahead to another gate, through which, turn right and walk by the wall to a final gate in the corner, coming out onto a lane. Turn left to return to Sprint Bridge and Burneside.

### Foxglove

*A common summer flower in the hedgerows and banks, its tall clusters of purple, or occasionally, creamy white, flowers appearing between June and August. Despite its attractive appearance, all parts of the plant are very poisonous, as it contains digitalis, which affects the heart. However, in his Complete Herbal, first published in 1653, the physician Nicholas Culpeper waxed ardently on its qualities, describing it as having a gentle and friendly nature. Amongst its uses, he suggested a deconcoction of the herb to cleanse and purge the body, both upwards and downwards, to cure the King's Evil or as a remedy for a scabby head.*

Other *Questa* Guides, published
and in production

**Walks with Children in the Lake District:**

Buttermere and the Vale of Lorton
Borrowdale
Patterdale
Around Coniston
Ambleside/Grasmere
Keswick and the Newlands Valley
Around Windermere

**More Walks with Children in the Lake District:**
Around Kendal

**Walks with Children in the Yorkshire Dales:**

Wharfedale
Swaledale and Wensleydale
Malham and Airedale